Living Beyond Check to MONDAY

A Spiritual Path to Wealth and Prosperity

Living Beyond Check to MONDAY

A Spiritual Path to Wealth and Prosperity

Lynn Richardson
"The Mortgage Guru"

With Contributions by Sonya Terry

Additional Books by Lynn Richardson

Living Check to Monday: The Real Deal About Money, Credit and Financial Security

Yes, You're Approved! The Real Deal About Getting a Mortgage and Buying a Home
By Lynn Richardson and Lori S. Jones Gibbs

Coming Soon . . .
Put On Your Financial Armor: End Your Battle with Money for Good

Requests for permission and other inquiries should be addressed to:

Publisher Name	Lynn Richardson Enterprises, Inc.
Publisher Address	PO Box 2815
Publisher City, State	Country Club Hills, IL 60478
Phone:	888.596.6123
Email:	dreamscometrue@lynnrichardson.com
Website:	www.lynnrichardson.com

ISBN 10:	0-9773232-1-8
ISBN 13:	978-0-9773232-1-0

Scripture taken from the HOLY BIBLE, NEW INTERNATIONAL VERSION®. NIV®. Copyright © 1973, 1978, 1984 by International Bible Study. Used by permission of Zondervan. All Rights Reserved.

KJV indicates Scripture quotations from the King James Version.

Do not let this Book depart from your mouth; meditate on it day and night, so that you may be careful to do everything written in it. Then you will be prosperous and successful.

Joshua 1:8 (NIV)

Living Beyond Check to MONDAY

A Spiritual Path to Wealth and Prosperity

Table of Contents

Acknowledgements

This was truly a task for me. I wrote the first book, essentially, in a weekend. This one took more than a year.

I even co-authored a third book, which I completed over the course of several days, before I completely finished this work. While the other two books were a testimony, this one manifested a breakthrough experience. Oh boy, did I cry, pray, scream, beg, believe, and most importantly, have FAITH. Without faith, this work could not have been completed. With out the experience and the testimony to demonstrate the faith, I could never have shared this breakthrough with you.

I thank God, who is the true author of this work. My hands and my life were simply used as a conduit for this message.

I thank my best friend and husband, Demietrius, for your love and support. This is our breakthrough!! I thank my daughters, Cydney, Taylor, and Kennedy who are the inspiration for my aspirations. I also thank my parents who gave me life, and my best girlfriend in the whole wide world, Grandma Bea, for nurturing my spirit and raising me.

I thank Sonya Terry, my sister, friend, and Soror, who shared her gift of healing with me and will share it with millions of readers worldwide. And I thank two additional very special Sorors / sister friends: Deadra Woods Stokes and Lori Jones Gibbs for your consistency and support.

Thank you, Pastor Bullock, for being a leader and a mentor, compassionate in your ministry and uncompromising in the manifestation of truth. You have had more of an impact on me than you know.

I thank Elder Stephon Henderson for warring on my behalf, and I thank my spiritual mother, Marva Nicholson, Reverend Howard S. Nichols (who will always be my Pastor in my heart), Lady Ruth Nichols, and the entire Pleasant Gift family.

I thank my Pastor and First Lady, Rev. Dr. Trunell D. Felder and Rev. Dr. Alexis L. Felder for their vision and love – it exudes from the pulpit into my life each and every day. I also thank my mentors Rev. Robbie Craig and Rev. Dr. Vera Stewart, my Kingdom Financial Ministry brothers and sisters, my adopted parents Brother and Sister Mundy, and my entire church family for giving me and my family a place to call our spiritual home.

To Readers Around the World: This book will compel you to DO. In other words, it is a book of action. You cannot read it and stay the same. You cannot experience it and do nothing. In the name of the one and only Christ Jesus, I am grateful for my breakthrough and am hopeful and prayerful that you will receive yours with unmitigated faith and humble thanksgiving. Amen.

Lynn Richardson

Acknowledgements

Lynn, I really treasure our special friendship. I am blessed to have you in my life. We are kindred spirits called to provide a higher level of support and service to the masses. I feel honored to be on this mission with you.

Heavenly father I thank you for the blessings that will come forth from this project. I thank you for the healing that will take place in the reader's heart. I thank you for the people that will turn each page and hear your voice – the voice of truth. I thank you for the process Lynn and I have undertaken to get to this space where we are willing and able to be of service to your divine plan. Thank you God. Thank you God. Thank you God. ....And so it is. Amen.

Sonya Terry

Living Beyond Check to MONDAY

A Spiritual Path to Wealth and Prosperity

Foreword

A Flame burns best when it is passed on! . . . An African Proverb.

When I first met Lynn Richardson, nearly six years ago, she and I were working in the corporate market place of America proclaiming the good news of minority home ownership and the necessity for African American and minority consumers to leverage their collective purchasing power of over two trillion dollars domestically. I knew from our first encounter that she was due for a promising career of advocacy and scholarship. Her passion, perceptiveness, and power of unique persuasion were clearly shaped upon the anvil of life's experiences from the academic environment at Northwestern University, Evanston, Illinois and the tough streets of Chicago, Illinois. Those who heard her weekly radio show, listened to her conference presentations or spoke with her in intimate settings, learned very quickly that Lynn Richardson has a prophetic call on her life. And as she would be the first to say, Lynn reluctantly accepted this call due to professional and societal constraints.

But now, she's unleashed her calling in her newest book, "***Living Beyond Check to Monday: A Spiritual Path to Wealth and Prosperity***," which declares that your giving allows for gain when you seek prosperity over poverty. The reader witnesses all of Lynn's passion, expertise and new revelation knowledge on personal financial growth, spiritual transformation and personal prosperity. This work identifies the inevitable synergy between abundant living, spiritual adherence and emotional liberation. So often these three categories of our lives are either neglected or disproportionately emphasized. Lynn argues that each individual must acknowledge that there is a biblical foundation for abundant life and economic prosperity. She challenges the readers to forsake the old Wall Street moniker, "greed is good," and embrace a new paradigm and personal mindset based upon Ten Prosperity Commandments.

Ever mindful of the most severe global financial collapse in our nation's history, coupled with unprecedented housing foreclosures, bank failures, double digit job unemployment within minority communities, record governmental deficits in the trillions of dollars, and the destruction of retirement dreams, Lynn Richardson offers us the audacity of hope in the midst of all these apparent crises. She has now compiled perhaps her finest work yet, "*A Spiritual path to Wealth and Prosperity*", to serve as a pathway to renewal and restoration for all who read these pages. The genre of this prophetic call is reminiscent of the biblical prophets who seized the moment and proclaimed a more excellent way for God's people who were accustomed to walking in darkness versus embracing the light of wisdom, knowledge, liberation and ultimate success.

Lynn lovingly invites those who are seeking spiritual liberation from personal debt and financial confusion to walk with her through this spiritual pathway and personal financial journey. For this journey, with its unique 'exit signs' – *The Foundation for Prosperity; Your Healing; Ten Prosperity Commandments; and Your Daily Walk* – leads to practical exercises and strategies that the reader must undertake to achieve the abundant life that awaits us in the end. As the reader engages in journaling, meditation and scriptural memorization, wisdom wealth is manifested for righteous living.

Whether you're a part of a small group bible study session, reading it because you hope to start a new venture or business enterprise, or contemplating speaking on the subject of financial literacy and personal growth development, *Living Beyond Check to Monday: A Spiritual Path to Wealth and Prosperity* will help you realize your ultimate dream of prosperity and peace. I pray that eyes of understanding of all who read this book be opened and that your hearts be warmed by the grace God has given unto Lynn in this anointed and prophetic work. Thank you, Lynn, for this labor of love given to all who read these pages. May God's richest and choicest blessings be upon all who read it.

Hon. Rev. Larry S. Bullock, [Retired Member of Illinois House of Representatives]
Founder, Senior Pastor and Teacher: Living Faith Cathedral Worship Center, Barrington, Illinois

Living Beyond Check to MONDAY

A Spiritual Path to Wealth and Prosperity

Introduction: The Source of Wealth & Prosperity

"It is easier for a camel to go through the eye of a needle, than for a rich man to enter into the kingdom of God." **Mark 10:25 (KJV)**

So you mean to tell me that a big 900 pound camel has a better chance of squeezing through Madea's sewing needle than a rich man getting into heaven?

Okay, I know what you're thinking . . . unless there are some microscopic sized camels running around in the desert, there is no way I can achieve my dream of becoming wealthy AND earning enough brownie points to get into heaven. The Bible says so. But I need money. And I'll be honest. I need more than a little . . . I need more than enough . . . I want some extra! Yes, I want to be wealthy. I want to be rich! What's wrong with that? I mean, look at Oprah! I have a good heart, too. I'll even take care of grandma, give to the needy, feed the poor, and yes, I'll even start tithing!

If you're like me, you've even started to break down the scripture. Okay, the Lord said "easier for a camel," but He didn't say it is "impossible for the rich," because if he meant "impossible," he would have said "impossible," so if I can just find a way for a camel to get through the eye of a needle – easily -- then I can certainly justify striking it rich AND getting into heaven. Right?

Wrong!

Like so many other passages in the bible, this one is often misunderstood. It's misunderstood like our money is misunderstood. For if we read before and after the scripture, we will understand the true meaning of the camel and needle business.

Mark 10:17, 19-25 (KJV)
17 And when he was gone forth into the way, there came one running, and kneeled to him, and asked him, Good Master, what shall I do that I may inherit eternal life? **19 Thou knowest the commandments, Do not commit adultery, Do not kill, Do not steal, Do not bear false witness, Defraud not, Honour thy father and mother.** *20 And he answered and said unto him, Master, all these have I observed from my youth. 21 Then Jesus beholding him loved him, and said unto him,* **One thing thou lackest: go thy way, sell whatsoever thou hast, and give to the poor, and thou shalt have treasure in heaven: and come, take up the cross, and follow me.** *22 And he was sad at that saying, and went away grieved: for he had great possessions. 23 And Jesus looked round about, and saith unto his disciples,* **How hardly shall they that have riches enter into the kingdom of God!** *24 And the disciples were astonished at his words. But Jesus answereth again, and saith unto them,* **Children, how hard is it for them that <u>trust</u> in riches to enter into the kingdom of God! 25 It is easier for a camel to go through the eye of a needle, than for a rich man to enter into the kingdom of God.** *26 And they were astonished out of measure, saying among themselves, Who then can be saved?*

Okay, here's the **<u>Living Beyond Check to Monday</u>** version:

Malcolm	Jesus, I've decided that I want to live forever. What do I need to do?
Jesus	You know the rules. No cheating on your wife, no killing people, no stealing, no lying, no cheating people out of their stuff . . . and of course, you must respect Mom and Dad.

Introduction: The Source of Wealth & Prosperity

Malcolm	That's all? I've been following all of the rules since I was young. So, I'm cool, right?
Jesus	Well, you know I would love for you to live forever with Me and My Father, but you're missing something. You have too much stuff. You won't need all of that in Heaven. So go and sell your cars, houses, clothes . . . sell everything. Take the money you earn from selling your stuff and give it all to the homeless shelter, 'cause I got your back in Heaven, and when you come back, you can follow me. Just do what I do. Then you can live forever with Me and My Father.
Malcolm	(silence) (Malcolm walked away very, very sad . . . thinking about all of his stuff)
Jesus	(exasperated, he turns to the Disciples) Rich people won't make it to Heaven!
Disciples	(Silence and Shock!)
Jesus	(After seeing that the Disciples are in shock) What I meant to say is, people who **trust** in riches will hardly make it to Heaven. I could put a camel through the eye of a needle quicker than a rich man could get into Heaven.
Disciples	(The Disciples, still in shock, mumble to each other) Well, if that's the criteria, who can be saved?

Even after Jesus explained that those who "trust in riches" (and not rich people) would have a hard time getting into heaven, the disciples remained in a state of shock. So, I must conclude that some of the disciples were, in fact, rich. I imagine that some of the disciples wore nice garments and shoes and lived in nice homes. I imagine that some of the disciples had an abundance of food, land and livestock. I imagine that some of the disciples had enough money to buy the "$14-dollars-a-pail-pre-cleaned" chitlins instead of the "$5-dollars-a-pail-its-gonna-take-three-days-to-clean" chitlins.

I imagine that some of the disciples had enough money to buy ground turkey instead of 50% lean ground beef. I imagine that at least one of the disciples had money stashed away for many rainy days to come. I imagine that some of the disciples had rich cousins and rich daddies and they began to think of all the people who would not make it to heaven because "trust in riches" would ultimately disqualify them.

And I would imagine that some of the disciples realized, at that very moment, that they, too, may have been guilty of trusting in riches.

Like the man who wanted eternal life in the scripture, how many times in our lives have we demonstrated our trust in money over our trust in God? I mean, let's be honest. If the Lord came down right now and told you to sell everything, give the money away, and come follow Him, would **you** make it to heaven? How many times have we prayed to God for a miracle to bail us out of an emergency and we get the money, we fail to tithe, fail to save, fail to share, and fail to change the very behavior that had us on our knees begging for a miracle in the first place?

How many times have we said, when I start making more money, I'm going to help my church? Or even worse, when I get my money right, I'll start GOING to church? When I get on my feet, I'll start saving. When the Lord blesses me with a new job, I'll start paying the bill collectors, even though I buy exotic coffee twice a day (reality check: any coffee that costs several dollars PER CUP is exotic in my book!).

When, when, when . . . sad to say, but every time we add a "when" clause, then we are demonstrating our trust in money and unfortunately, that means a whole lot of camels will be going through needles.

That also means we keep living from check to Monday.

You know, like I described in the other book. The CTM Syndrome: get paid on Friday, kick it on the weekends, pay "something on" the past due bills, and by Monday, we're broke! Then we pray, cry, worry, and do whatever it takes to get to the next payday and the cycle repeats itself.

So what do we do about it? What are **you** going to do about it? I think the scripture makes it plain and clear. We must replace our trust in riches with an unshakeable trust in God in order to achieve true wealth.

But in order to trust something, we must understand it. So, like my first book, you bought this one out of desperation, borrowed it from a friend, or maybe you got it as a part of Bible study. The point is, you have it now. So pray for understanding, stay committed to a spiritual path to wealth and prosperity, and let's just hope and pray that we don't hear of any camels going through needles before we are transformed!

Part 1

The Foundation for Wealth & Prosperity

The Pre-Requisite for Prosperity

"A feast is made for laughter, and wine maketh merry; but money answereth all things." (Ecc 10:19) **KJV**

I know what you're thinking   This wealth and prosperity business is tricky! First we find out that Christ believes a camel will get through a needle before a rich man will go to heaven, so I kind of decide I don't want to be rich, and now you're saying "money answers all things" and now I want to be rich again!

And I'm not supposed to trust money!

Right?

Correct. In order to understand this one, "money answereth all things," we have to go behind the scenes. Let's consider an example we can easily understand.

Just imagine, for example, that every living being needs cow's milk in order to sustain life. So, "Cow's Milk is the Answer to Life." No need for immunizations, food, chicken, mother's milk, water, vitamins, steak, formula, or seafood. If you get sick, just get some extra cow's milk. Cow's milk is it. Without cow's milk, we would all, unfortunately, die. Cow's milk answers all physical things. So cow's milk is what we need to nurture, love, understand, and focus our attention on, right?

Wrong!

Without healthy cows producing healthy milk, there would be no milk to sustain life in the first place. So the "cow", which is the provider of the "cow's milk," is what we need to nurture, love, understand, and focus our attention on. Not the milk itself.

Got it? I know you do . . .

But for the record, I am quite happy that the above example is just that – an example. I happen to like chicken wings, seafood, Honey Smacks cereal, Hawaiian Punch, and of course, Grandma's soul food!

Now, back to the point.

Let's apply the cow's milk example and instead of cow's milk, let's focus our attention on money.

We now know that "money answers all things" because the Holy Bible says so. We need money to live. We need money to live well. We even need money to die! But where does money come from?   The federal reserve? Alan Greenspan? Bill Gates . . . maybe? . . . of course not!

It comes from God! How do we know?

Because God created everything! He created the earth and everything in it.   Gold, silver, the federal reserve, and yes, even Bill Gates! It . . . we . . all belong to Him! *(See Psalm 24:1; Psalm 50: 10 – 12; Colossians 1:16)*

The Pre-Requisite for Prosperity

That includes money, too!

Since God is the provider of money, then it is our relationship with God that we need to nurture and focus our attention on – not the money or any other resource He provides.

So, I know what you're thinking . . . . If God owns and creates everything, then why do I have to tithe? Why do we have to give back ten percent if He created it all? Didn't He save some for Himself? (chuckle . . . go on and admit it . . . I know you have asked yourself this question!)

Well, let me put it this way. . . we have to tithe because OUR FATHER SAID SO! *(See Genesis 14:20; Deuteronomy 16:16 and 14:22-23 and 8:11-14; 2Chronicles 31:5,12; Proverbs 3:9; Malachi 3: 8 - 12)*

You know what I'm talking about. When you were little, your momma told you to do certain things and when you asked "Why?" she snapped back, "Because I said so!"

And you also know that you had selective memory. You easily complied with the things you liked (baby, yes, you can go outside) and you somehow forgot, disregarded, or down right disobeyed the things you did not like (but, you must clean your room).

And the conversation went something like this:

"Mommy, you said I could go outside and play."

"Yes pumpkin, but I also told you to clean your room."

"But I don't want to clean my room right now, I can do it before I go to bed tonight."

And the struggle begins. The struggle between momma's instructions and YOUR will.

Momma patiently tells you that you must do BOTH in order to receive your reward.

And if you were anything like me as a child, you started talking back to momma.

And if your momma was anything like my Grandma, your momma eventually lost her patience and you found yourself in the middle of a good butt whipping with a switch!

That's right, leaves and all!

Now back to the point.

Back to what the Father tells us to do via his Word, the Holy Bible.   We, too, try to pick and choose which orders we want to follow and which orders we don't or can't follow.

Command: "Love one another."

Response: I did that.

The Pre-Requisite for Prosperity

Command   "Honor your mother and father."

        Response: I did that.

Command: "Treat people how you want to be treated."

        Response: I did that.

Command: "Tithe ten percent of your earnings."
           (See Deuteronomy 14:22 – 23; Malachi 3: 8 – 12; Matthew 23:23; Genesis 14: 18 – 20)

        Response: *"I need some more money. I don't have enough money to even pay bills. I need a better job. I don't know what the church is doing with my money.*

        We have more excuses than a man going to jail.

        I'll start when I get back from vacation. I can't tithe off of my tax refund! Or my bonus! Or my social security check!"

        And the most stubborn of us just decide all together that we are not going to tithe at all regardless of how much money we have!

        "That's a man-made law. That was in the Old Testament. My church doesn't need my money. My pastor is living better than half of the ministry, combined. I don't even go to church, I'm an at-home Christian."

And when we start talking back to God and operating in disobedience, the spiritual whipping begins.

You're not sure what this whipping looks like? Oh, let me help you!

You know you're being whipped by the Father when no matter how many bills you choose NOT to pay, you still end up broke. I mean, isn't that an oxymoron? If you're not paying ANY bills, and you're earning money, you should have plenty of money stashed away, right?

Wrong! When you don't do what you're told, God puts holes in your pockets. Since you won't do what you're supposed to do, you lose the wisdom and the ability to retain and grow your money in a responsible way. *(See Malachi 3:8 – 12)*

You know you're being whipped when you make more money each year on your job, but have less to show for it.

You know you're being whipped when you see people who become rich, win the lottery, get a movie deal, or otherwise fall into "big money" . . . and you see those same people on drugs, in divorce court, running from one relationship to the next, walking around with a bad attitude, shaving their hair off their heads, going into seclusion, losing all their money, and filing bankruptcy soon after.

The Pre-Requisite for Prosperity

I don't know about you, but I will take a whipping from momma any day. When daddy gets involved, it seems to hurt just a little bit more, right?

You know I'm right. And I know you get the point.

The point is this, if we don't honor the source of the blessing, the blessing sours. If we don't take care of those cows, then the cow will produce sour milk! If we are not obedient in our tithing, giving and other spiritual laws related to wealth and prosperity, then the money we have ultimately sours and becomes less capable of assisting us in living out our purpose in God's kingdom.

Tithing is physical evidence that God truly is first in our lives.

So the question we must ask ourselves is this: What does the evidence show?

Am I living check to Monday?

Or, am I lucky enough to make it from check to check?

Or, do I have a 6 months emergency reserve fund?

Or, am I on my way to a wealthy and spirit-filled life with unshakeable evidence of my trust in God?

Because "money answereth all things," then what we choose to do with our money becomes the evidence of our faith (or lack thereof) in God to supply our needs and those choices demonstrate our obedience to His will.

And because tithing, undergirded by faith, is an act of obedience, then tithing is a physical manifestation of our relationship with God as our ultimate Source and Provider.

The Temptation of Wealth

"When you ask, you do not receive, because you ask with wrong motives, that you may spend what you get on your pleasures." **(James 4:3) NIV**

Now, I know the Lord was speaking directly to me on this one. That is, in my past life of frivolous earning and spending. Weren't we told, "ask and you shall receive"? And haven't we gotten down on our knees many a night asking for virtually everything? "Lord I need a new car." "Lord I need some new furniture." "A new fur coat." That's the problem. It says it right there in the scripture. We ask and DO NOT receive because we waste money!

You know that's the truth!

Plus, more money causes more problems. Even the late Notorius BIG said so. The more money you get, the more Pookie and 'nem want to borrow. And you have a hard time saying "no".

The more money you get, the more stuff you want. The 2008 Lexus ES300 isn't enough, you HAVE to get the 2009. The more money you get, the more you depend on money as your foundation for independence. And unfortunately, the more money you get, the further many of us stray away from developing intimacy with God and the wisdom to maintain wealth.

"People who want to get rich fall into temptation and a trap and into many foolish and harmful desires that plunge men into ruin and destruction. For the love of money is a root of all kinds of evil. Some people, eager for money, have wandered from the faith and pierced themselves with many griefs" (1 Tim 6:9 – 10 NIV).

True wealth, however, comes with no problems and no worries added to it, as evidenced in **Proverbs 10:22**.

Having wealth without the Godly wisdom to dispense and preserve it properly is like placing a 5 year old over a Fortune 100 company. Yes, it's a huge billion dollar company, but it will plummet to bankruptcy in the hands and of someone who is unable to handle the great responsibility.

Can't you just see Jr. running this Fortune 100 company?

"I'm still tired from the weekend, so no work on Mondays. Tuesdays either. And everybody can go home early on Friday. Plus, we need some new video games. Stop making all these firewalls and stuff. We need more video games!"

Funny? Sure! But, we're just like Jr. when it comes to money and wealth.

"I'm still behind on my bills from last month, so no saving or tithing this pay period. Matter of fact, don't answer the telephone 'cause I don't feel like talking to any bill collectors. I need to go and get my nails and feet done so I can relax!"

And that's the temptation of wealth – spending unnecessarily.

The Temptation of Wealth

Spending out of order.

Spending without wisdom.

So how do we get in alignment with "wisdom" spending? It's quite simple. Live by the 10 – 10 – 30 – 50 rule as described in my first book, Living Check to Monday: The Real Deal About Money, Credit and Financial Security.

I will go over it very briefly here: Whenever you get any kind of money for any reason, this is how you will allocate those funds:

10 %   for Tithing
10%   for Saving
30%   Cash in your pocket for incidentals, groceries, gas, hair, etc.
50%   in your checking account for Bills

If there is not enough money for bills, guess what? You have a big problem! The good news is this – now you can see it on paper and fix it You will have to cut back in some areas. This will be discussed later in Prosperity Commandment #6.

If you have money left over in the bills category, "THIS IS NOT THE TIME TO START BUYING JOO-JOO'S!". You know what "joo-joos" are. It's all the stuff you don't need! Expensive shoes . . . *unnecessary* shoes . . . expensive clothes . . . *unnecessary* clothes . . . deals at the stake (like I described in the other book). Instead, if you have money left over in the bills category, you can do any one or all of the following:

1. Leave the money there, because you will have some annual or quarterly expenses that need your attention (real estate taxes, insurance premiums, membership dues, etc.);

2. Increase your saving (perhaps for vacation, retirement, education, or Christmas shopping);

3. Increase your investing and/or maximize your insurance and estate planning;

4. Increase your offerings, giving, and/or tithing;

I heard Joyce Meyers make this profound statement: "Everyone has two tests to pass in life as it relates to money: (1) What you do when you don't have enough money, and (2) What you do when you have more than enough noney." The problem with some of us is that we are still in Financial Kindergarten and even though we have the answers to the test (Scripture), we still can't get to first grade, high school or college! The point is this: when you can demonstrate that you can be trusted with little, you will be blessed with and trusted with much more. *(See Luke 16: 10 – 13)*

And when God trusts you and then blesses you with more, you will be spiritually convicted to nurture this trust with discipline, wisdom and financial choices that are in alignment with His will for your life. Ultimately, the key to overcoming the temptation of wealth is understanding this basic truth:

The Temptation of Wealth

More money will never solve a money problem.

If it could, millionaires and billionaires wouldn't go bankrupt!

There are three things that work in unison to solve a money problem:

1. **Healing** - which is addressed in Part 2 of this book;

2. **Discipline** – which is introduced and reinforced in Part 3 of this book; and

3. **Spiritual Wisdom** as manifested in the Holy Scriptures (there are scriptural references throughout this journey).

Now, let's walk together along the *Spiritual Path to Wealth and Prosperity*.

Part 2

Your Healing
By Sonya Terry

The processes outlined in this book will work for you when they are followed as prescribed. However, in order to experience the true "break through" intended by the author, first we need to identify the barriers that hold you back.

This section focuses on recognizing how your money and overall prosperity is connected to your ability to have spiritual balance in your life and healing is the key to removing the barriers that block the flow of money and prosperity.

True Prosperity

Many of us wonder why money seems to slip through our fingers and why others continue to prosper when we continue to struggle. Some have a surplus of money in the bank and their career is on track, but their relationships are suffering. You can have the luxury car and an exquisite home but secretly suffer from addiction, depression, insecurity or a broken heart. When one area of your life comes together it may seem as if another is falling apart.

True prosperity is more than money. Prosperity is also an abundance of health, peace, harmony and love. You become balanced and live in a space of spiritual, mental, physical and emotional integrity.

You are the sum total of your thoughts and feelings. Your thinking and emotions drive your actions and reactions and both are sources of energy.

When your thoughts, words, actions and reactions are aligned and reflect self actualization, then you have achieved true prosperity. You know who you are and are comfortable in your skin. You are at peace with the world.

Jesus said, *"I am come that they might have life, and that they might have it more abundantly"* (John 10:10 KJV). The abundant life is about prosperity. It is where all your needs and wants are fulfilled because they are one in the same.

Life is challenging us to do and be so much more than just acquire dollars and cents. Of course there is nothing wrong with acquiring things, but never lose your perspective -- remember things should not define you -- always remember who you are.

Who are you? Write your answer, in your own words, in the space below:

_____

_____

_____

_____

_____

_____

_____

You Are Spirit!

*Y*ou were born in the image and likeness of God. There is so much more to you than flesh and blood. You are multifaceted. Your spiritual, mental, physical and emotional self are connected. Although we try to compartmentalize aspects of our nature and make them amenable to the situations of life, the universe will not tolerate it. We are called to be perfectly balanced.

There are aspects of your being that are strong. You have natural talents and gifts which help you succeed and accomplish anything you have set out to accomplish. There are also aspects of your being that are weak, which is the reason why we have challenges. Challenges come to strengthen your spiritual muscles.

The emotional aspect of you includes your passion, hurt, anger, joy, peace, fear, faith and love. Your emotional self houses the memories of your past.

The mental aspect of you is logical, reasoning, analytical and intellectual. Problems in this area manifest as confusion, frustration and an inability to focus your energy.

The physical aspect of you is more than just your body. It also includes your finances, relationships, goals, acquisitions, career and family.

The spiritual aspect is where your divine inspiration, creativity, discernment and healing reside. It also houses the spirit of God. It is the Christ within and the reason why God is with you every minute, every hour of every day.

Please list below at least one strength in each area:

Emotional
_____

_____

Mental
_____

_____

Physical
_____

_____

Spiritual
_____

_____

Barriers to Prosperity

Where am I going with this? It is very common to have barriers that prevent you from experiencing true prosperity. The barriers may have nothing to do with your finances. A barrier may exist in the emotional and mental aspects of your life and manifest in the physical aspect.

In other words, when you have problems in your relationships, they can filter over into your finances. When you feel stifled and unfulfilled in your career, your relationships may be effected. Financial problems may lead to severe health issues. Basically, if you think the unresolved negative drama of your romantic relationships, divorce, family issues, poor health, hurt, frustration, fear or anger are not affecting other aspects of your life…think again.

We try to compartmentalize those aspects of our lives that are not working and pretend they are separate entities and not connected to who and what we are.

Think again. You are and always will be the common denominator of your world. Everything happens for a reason. You know there is a lesson for **you** in these situations because **you** keep showing up.

In other words you will continue to attract people and situations that make you uncomfortable until you get the lesson. Rather than viewing the situation from a victim's perspective, such as "why do bad things always happen to me", consider it as an opportunity to grow and become a better person. Once you have learned the lesson the person or situation will no longer have the same effect on you. You will be able to move on to bigger and better things. If you choose not to move on, then you will remain in the cycle of pain, insecurity, anger, etc. indefinitely.

Please list below at least one barrier in each area:

Emotional
_____

_____

Mental
_____

_____

Physical
_____

_____

Spiritual
_____

_____

Healing

*W*e were created to be perfect, whole and complete in the eyes of God. Your challenges are "custom made" to help you to reach your ultimate potential and deal with what is not working.

When you ignore an aspect of your life, let's say the physical aspect, and purely focus on the material or emotional aspects of your life, at some point you will be required to take a closer look at what you have been denying.

So what do you need?

You need . . . I need . . . we all need . . . healing.

What is healing? Webster's dictionary defines healing as "restoration to original purity". I believe health is a by-product of healing and healing is restoration to God's perfect pattern. Our spiritual self is perfect. It is the part of us that never gets sick or needs Tylenol. You were created "in the beginning" by God's perfect idea of himself hence, *"Then God said, Let us make man in our image, in our likeness, and let them rule over the fish of the sea and the birds of the air, over the livestock, over all the earth, and over all the creatures that move along the ground"* (Genesis 1:26 NIV). God's perfect image exists within us.

If we are perfect, then "what is the problem?" Why do we have difficulties in our lives in the form of poor relationships, too much debt, too little cash, sickness, low self esteem, abuse and crime? The list goes on and on. Most people believe they need to approach these issues at the surface level but the permanent solution resides in our ability to tap into the spiritual depths and aspect of our being. What you really need.....is healing. You need to release and let go of the mental and emotional barriers that hold you back.

True healing begins in the mind. Your breakthrough begins in your mind. Basically, you need to change your mind. When you change your thoughts and emotions about a situation the healing follows. It doesn't matter what the situation is. The healing process is the same because the only thing you will ever heal is the mental and emotional condition affecting the physical aspects of your life.

Everything that is happening in your life is a result of what is going on in your mind and emotions. In fact, your body exists in your mind. I am sure you have heard of the "mind-body connection". Modern medicine is acknowledging and demonstrating how people are improving their clinical outcomes with the help of positive inspirational messages, including prayer.

I can understand if you are not consciously aware of what needs to be healed because your body has an amazing defense mechanism to pain, it is called denial and yes, it is not just a river.

Denial is your body's psychological way of not facing your pain. Nevertheless, you will attract situations to give you a clue that something is wrong. Again, this is the reason why many people have cycles in their lives of experiencing the same disappointments. The people may be different but the underlying situation is the same.

Six Basic Steps to Healing

There are many approaches to healing. I have included six basic steps that are designed to help you release the barriers that hold you back mentally, emotionally and physically.

1.   Ask yourself, "Do I want to be healed?"

This is the question Jesus asked throughout his ministry and it is an important one. Many times people say they want a healing but in actuality they want attention and use their problems as a way of getting the attention they so desperately need, hence the "drama kings and queens of the world."

Others are so attached to their pain it defines who they are. This is evident in people who continue the cycle of abuse. This is also seen in people who say they want a healing but are not willing to take the necessary steps that bring about permanent healing.

If you are willing to do whatever it takes to express your healing, ask God for the strength to make it happen.

So, do you want to be healed? Yes   or   No   (circle one)

If you answered "Yes," in the space below, write "I want to be healed because . . . . "

_____

_____

_____

_____

If you answered "No," and are not ready to face or acknowledge what is holding you back, know that everything is in divine order and when you are ready to move on your healing will take place.

Perhaps acknowledging that you need to be healed brings back too many buried memories and tears. It is okay to cry. Crying is a form of cleansing and helps remove toxic emotional energy from the body. Take the time to acknowledge your feelings knowing that "this too shall pass." The goal is to get "through" this state and not stay stuck in it any longer than you have to.

Say this prayer,

"Father, I know that I need to be healed in this area, but I am not ready. Please give me the strength to release this situation and move to the perfect place of peace that you have planned for me. Amen."

Say this prayer as much as you need to until you can answer "Yes, I am ready to be healed".

2.   Believe.

*Y*ou have to know that you can be free! "Fear not, little flock; for it is your Father's good pleasure to give you the kingdom." (Luke 12:32 King James Version) You need to believe that God is on your side. If Jesus came so that we can have an abundant life, ask yourself are you living the abundant life? If you are not, then you need a healing. If you are living a total and complete abundant life then you are here to teach others how to get there and I submit to you that once you have "arrived", there will be other challenges for you to face.

Why?

Your soul must continue to grow and unfold. God created us to grow from human awareness to spiritual consciousness. You were born to evolve. Everything God created has the ability to evolve.

As long as you have a body, it means there is something left in this world for you to do, teach or experience in this world. KEEP LIVING.

Believe, the situation has no power over you. Believe you can have the things your heart desire. Believe that you and God are a majority there is no thing or person standing in your way.

Do you believe you can be free?   Yes   or   No   (circle one)

In the space below, write "I believe being free will allow me to . . .

_____

_____

_____

_____

_____

_____

_____

_____

Six Basic Steps to Healing

3.   Identify what you are healing.

*Y*ou can't repair what you won't face. If you are not aware of what needs to be healed, ask yourself, "What gives me the most emotional pain, worry, anger or grief?" This the answer you have been looking for. If you are still unsure, ask God and the first thing that comes to mind is usually it.

Clarity is a beautiful thing. Once you are clear on the issue it is easier to release it.

Answer the question, "What areas/issues give me the most emotional pain, worry, anger or grief?"

_____

_____

_____

_____

_____

_____

_____

_____

_____

_____

_____

_____

4. You must forgive.

*N*egative feelings and emotions are indicative of the need to forgive. Your feelings are a barometer of what needs to be healed. When people "push your buttons" they show you what you need to work on, which is why the buttons exist. Once you are healed no one can "push your buttons".

Pay attention to how you feel in certain situations. Don't be so quick to shut down your emotions and say "I'll get over it", "I don't care" or use other coping mechanisms.

When you are focusing on forgiveness you don't have to release the person. You must release your thoughts and negative feelings about the person. It is not about the other person or letting them "off the hook". It is about being empowered to move your life forward without excess mental or emotional baggage.

Take the time to commune with the Holy Spirit. You know you have forgiven and released the situation when you no longer have the negative feelings associated with the situation.

Forgiveness is all about you. No matter how hard you try to ignore it, negative emotions create a sense of disharmony and can result in "dis – ease" in your physical body among other things. Any disease in your body will ultimately destroy your physical, mental, and/or spiritual health. Harboring negative emotions simply is not worth it.

How many times do we forgive? The bible says we must forgive seventy seven times seven. This means you must forgive until you are completely clear of the situation. It is a process.

*W*ho do you need to forgive? (write as many people, entities or situations that cause anger, anxiety, worry, depression, hate, grief, or any other negative emotion as you can – for example, friends, family, past jobs, colleagues, spouses, old relationship partners, and yourself).

I need to forgive . . .

_____

_____

_____

_____

Six Basic Steps to Healing

Exercise- Forgiveness Meditation

1. Relax and place your feet a couple of inches apart on the floor.

2. Have your thumb, forefinger and middle finger touching. This creates a circuit of energy.

3. Place your hands in your lap.

4. Close your eyes, inhale and exhale three times

5. Hold the inhale for 5 seconds. Breathe normally. Repeat.

6. Imagine the person or situation you need to forgive.

7. Speak the following words as many times as you need.

I forgive you. I release you. I forgive myself. I am ready to move on knowing everything is in divine order. I am at peace with this situation. Thank you God.

Six Basic Steps to Healing

5.   Exercise your Faith.

$\mathcal{D}$emonstrate that you know your healing has taken place. If there is a person you need to call, pick up the telephone and make the call. If there is a letter that you need to write, write it. You don't have to mail the letter if you are not ready. Writing the letter can be therapeutic. If there is a budget that you need to create, do it. Faith is important because it helps the universe respond to your request and solidifies your healing in your own mind.

For every person or situation listed under "I need to forgive" in step 4, ask yourself, **"What do I need to do or say to be totally free of this situation?"** Maybe you need to write a letter, pay a visit, or just pray and move on. Do not second guess yourself. Listen to your first mind. Write the answers below.

1. _____

2. _____

3. _____

4. _____

5. _____

6. _____

7. _____

8. _____

9. _____

10. _____

11. _____

12. _____

13. _____

14. _____

15. _____

6.   Prayer and Thanksgiving.

*T*he final step in the process is to give thanks for your healing by repeating this prayer.

> *I choose love today. I choose to be free today. I release this situation to the healing power of the Holy Spirit. My heart is filled with love. I choose to be whole. This situation has no power over me. I no longer want to hold on to anything that doesn't make me strong. I accept my healing right here, right now. I accept my healing right here, right now. The past is the past. I am no longer a prisoner. I am free. It is finished. I look forward to my future, which is filled with the love of God and everything that is good. The Holy Spirit has healed me and everything is in Divine Order. Thank you God. I am perfect, whole and complete.*

Healing is the key to living a perfectly balanced and complete life.   Healing is the vehicle to overcoming adversity.

Healing makes the difference between "a minor setback" and years of living in a dysfunctional and destructive pattern. It is the antibiotic that removes the disease from your body and it brings about permanent results.

When you are truly healed of a thing, you are free to experience all the blessings life has in store for you. Embrace your healing and everything else will fall into place.

I am healed of the following:

_____

_____

_____

I still need healing in this (these) area(s) and I will continue my healing process:

_____

_____

_____

Part 3

Ten Prosperity Commandments
Walking Out God's Prosperity Wisdom

When most of us think of "wealth," we instantly think of "money." So we attempt to acquire more wealth by acquiring more money. Rarely do we try to acquire wisdom and Godly counsel along with the money, and we soon learn that acquiring money without wisdom and Godly counsel leads to bad consequences.

Prosperity, on the other hand, has a direct implication to Godly counsel, good health, happiness, peace, and yes . . . maybe even money. Dr. Cindy Trim defines success as the state of living in your divine purpose and she says you have achieved prosperity when you have enough money to support your needs and more than enough to give away as the Lord leads you.

So in part 2, we will review 10 Prosperity Commandments, discover their biblical foundation and complete exercises that will enable us to achieve the wealth and prosperity that God has planned for us as we live our daily lives within the confines of His divine purpose and will.

Ten Prosperity Commandments

*Y*our Spiritual Path to Wealth and Prosperity - **HOW TO READ THIS SECTION:**

a. **The Individual Walk: 12 Weeks**. Read Parts 1 and 2 as quickly as you wish. Do not read Part 3 in one sitting. Each prosperity commandment should be implemented over the course of one week (seven days) – unless otherwise noted -- to provide time for application into your life. If you think you are already following the prosperity commandments, remember that there is always room for improvement, so please do not rush through this section.

b. **The Group Walk: 6 Weeks**. Part 1 and 2 should be read prior to the first meeting or during the first 30 minutes of the first meeting. The remaining 5 meetings should cover Parts 3 and 4, with a review of 2 commandments per meeting. Participants should complete the commandments PRIOR to that week's meeting in order to receive maximum impact and engage in group discussion.

c. **The Conference Walk**. The best impact will be obtained by inviting the Author to facilitate this workshop. If this book is being used as a part of a workshop or conference, then it is acceptable to complete Part 3 in the course of a workshop (providing attendees have had an opportunity to read Part 1 and Part 2 prior to the beginning of the session), WITH GROUP DISCUSSION, but please try to have a break between each section.

Format for Each Prosperity Commandment:

d. **The Word: Understanding the Basics:** This section of each commandment will give you an opportunity to review scripture that provides the foundation for that particular commandment. The question and answer format allows you to apply your knowledge and interact with this process and/or your study group.

e. **The Word: Perfecting Your Prosperity Path:** This section provides you an opportunity to review scripture to strengthen your foundation. This is optional, but HIGHLY RECOMMENDED. You may choose to complete The Walk and The Wisdom and then come back to this section, or you may skip this section altogether and come back to it for reinforcement after you complete the entire book. It is up to you. What you choose to do here will impact your spiritual prosperity breakthrough.

f. **The Walk**: This section brings you face to face with your own situation with the expectation that your behavior will improve. If you are honest with yourself, you will cry, pray, scream, ask for forgiveness and/or rejoice. I have experienced all of these emotions. No matter how hard this gets, press forward and complete each walk IN ITS ENTIRETY. Your breakthrough is on the other side!

g. **The Wisdom**: I heard a quote once: *"Thoughts disentangle themselves when they pass through your fingertips."* Accordingly, this section guides you in journaling your experience and reflecting on how the Word and the Walk have impacted you and others around you. If you are not accustomed to writing, it's okay. Whatever you write, you will be transformed by the words you see looking back at you. A miracle is about to take place – so you want to document each and every step.

Answer each question honestly and address each issue promptly. You cannot fix what you will not face. If you feel any guilt or inadequacies, then pray for the spirit of Godly sorrow, repent and move on. Now is not the time to beat up on yourself. This is the time to walk in prosperity!

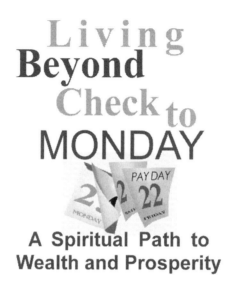

**A Spiritual Path to
Wealth and Prosperity**

"All the nations will be gathered before him, and he will separate the people one from another as a shepherd separates the sheep from the goats. He will put the sheep on his right and the goats on his left.

"Then the King will say to those on his right, 'Come, you who are blessed by my Father; take your inheritance, the kingdom prepared for you since the creation of the world. For I was hungry and you gave me something to eat, I was thirsty and you gave me something to drink, I was a stranger and you invited me in."

(Matthew 25: 32 – 35 NIV)

Prosperity Commandment #1
Give To Those Who Are Less Fortunate

Worldly Habits: Many of us believe we have to earn a certain amount to give. Some of us believe that the poor are there because of their own mistakes and those of us who have "made it" have no obligation to the poor. An finally, some of us have the ability and the desire to give . . . but we don't for one reason or another.

Prosperity Wisdom: Give more than you receive and support the weak. Jesus GAVE his life to redeem us from our dying condition. And God "so loved the world that he GAVE his only begotten son." (John 3:16). Giving and self-less "love" go hand in hand.

THE WORD: Understanding the Basics

Acts 20:35: Who must we help?

_____

_____

Acts 20:35: What did the Lord Jesus say?

_____

_____

Prov 31:20: Who helped the poor and the needy?

_____

_____

2 Cor 8: 7: In what six things should we excel?

_____

_____

2 Cor 9: 6 What are the rules for sowing and reaping?

_____

_____

2 Cor 9: 7 How are we to give and why?

_____

_____

Prosperity Commandment #1
Give To Those Who Are Less Fortunate

THE WORD: PERFECTING YOUR PROSPERITY PATH (optional)

Notes from Deuteronomy 15: 10 - 11

_____

_____

Notes from Proverbs 11:25 and Proverbs 22:9

_____

_____

Notes from Luke 6:38

_____

_____

Notes from Matthew 25: 32 - 46

_____

_____

Notes from Acts 10: 1 - 4

_____

_____

Notes from James 2: 14 - 16

_____

_____

Notes from 1 Timothy 6: 18 - 19

_____

_____

Prosperity Commandment #1
Give To Those Who Are Less Fortunate

THE WALK

1. What person or entity can you identify that needed your help within the few past weeks or months, yet you failed to provide assistance within your means?

_____

_____

2. How do you feel now, knowing that you could have provided assistance, but you didn't (because you forgot, failed to sacrifice, or dismissed the need)?

_____

_____

3. List at least one person/entity who will benefit from your resources (time, love, money, material possessions) over the next seven days.

_____

_____

4. List what resource you will provide (time, love, money, material possessions) and be specific.

_____

_____

5. You have seven days to complete steps 1 through 4 above.

Prosperity Commandment #1
Give To Those Who Are Less Fortunate

THE WISDOM:

Use this space to journal your Walk for Prosperity Commandment #1. Describe (1) what you did, (2) how it impacted others, (3) how it impacted you, and (4) what you plan to do moving forward.

(1) What you did:

_____

_____

_____

(2) How it impacted others (what happened, how did they respond):

_____

_____

_____

(3) How it impacted you (what truth, pain, joy, or freedom did you experience):

_____

_____

_____

(4) What you plan to do moving forward:

_____

_____

_____

(5) Write the scripture(s) that impacted you the most, remember it and share it with at least one other person this week.

_____

_____

_____

Living
Beyond
Check to
MONDAY

A Spiritual Path to
Wealth and Prosperity

Prosperity Commandment #2
Live Within Your Means

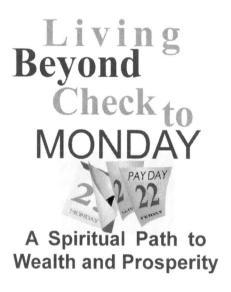

A Spiritual Path to Wealth and Prosperity

"One man pretends to be rich, yet has nothing; another pretends to be poor, yet has great wealth.
(Proverbs 13:7 NIV)

Prosperity Commandment #2
Live Within Your Means

Worldly Habits: Stop trying to "keep up with the Jones," avoid materialism, and stop trying to impress others. Our culture dictates that we must show the world we have wealth whenever we get the slightest bit of money. Moreover, we tend to "buy" relationships, friendships, and favor with other humans by impressing them with our wealth. We pay for things for others that we know we can't afford. We lend money to others then get desperately frustrated when they don't pay us back because we really couldn't afford to lend in the first place. We buy luxurious items like cars and furniture to win favor with envious onlookers. All of this leads to a life of confusion, facilitates the manifestation of low self esteem, and builds relationships that are based on lies, deceit, perception, and material wealth.

Prosperity Wisdom: Neither friendships nor self-esteem can be purchased. You will never have enough money to buy favor among humans. You will never have enough money to purchase items that will make you feel good about yourself – there will always be something missing; you will always need another "thing." Live below your means so you will enjoy peace. Remember, only the people who **don't matter** care what you have; because the people who **truly matter** . . . don't care!

THE WORD: Understanding the Basics

Acts 8:18 – 19: What was Simon trying to buy?

_____

_____

Acts 8: 20 - 21: What was Peter's response?

_____

_____

James 4:3: Why do we often fail to receive what we ask for?

_____

_____

1 Tim 6: 9 – 10 : What five things befall people who want to get rich and are eager for money?

_____

_____

Matthew 6:28 - 33: What do we receive as a result of seeking God's kingdom first?

_____

_____

Prosperity Commandment #2
Live Within Your Means

THE WORD: PERFECTING YOUR PROSPERITY PATH (optional)

Notes from Prov 13: 7

_____

_____

Notes from 1 Tim 6: 17 – 19:

_____

_____

Prosperity Commandment #2
Live Within Your Means

THE WALK

1. List at least one material possession that is above your means (in other words, you know you cannot afford to pay for this; you have had trouble meeting this obligation more than once in the past 12 months; or there are cheaper ways to obtain the same benefit from this possession while allowing you to prosper in other areas).

_____

_____

2. Who has paid a compliment or been impressed with your material possessions?

_____

_____

3. Do you have at least 6 months of monthly expenses saved in the bank for emergencies?

_____

_____

4 Who's more important, you or the person (people) listed in number 2?

_____

_____

5 How do you feel now, knowing the answer to number 1 through 4 above?

_____

_____

6. List, truthfully, what you must do in order to live within your means. Earning additional income is one way – but list this as an alternative. Face the truth about what you can do, based on what God has given you today, to immediately begin to operate within your means (trade in a car; take the bus; sell some clothes; cut credit cards, buy a cheaper home, etc.) Even if you do not do some of these things, write them down anyway so you will see in black and white what your options are.

_____

_____

_____

Prosperity Commandment #2
Live Within Your Means

THE WISDOM:

Use this space to journal your Walk for Prosperity Commandment #2. Describe (1) what you did, (2) how it impacted others, (3) how it impacted you, and (4) what you plan to do moving forward.

(1) What you did:

_____

_____

_____

(2) How it impacted others (what happened, how did they respond):

_____

_____

_____

(3) How it impacted you (what truth, pain, joy, or freedom did you experience):

_____

_____

_____

(4) What you plan to do moving forward:

_____

_____

_____

(5) Write the scripture(s) that impacted you the most, remember it and share it with at least one other person this week.

_____

_____

_____

Living
Beyond
Check to
MONDAY

A Spiritual Path to
Wealth and Prosperity

Prosperity Commandment #3
Save and Invest

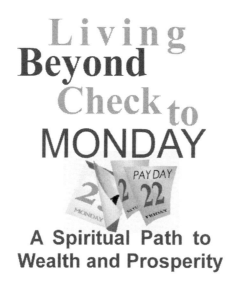

"*You have planted much, but have harvested little. You eat, but never have enough. You drink but never have your fill. You put on clothes but are not warm. You earn wages, only to put them in a purse with holes in it.*"
(Haggai 1: 5 – 6 NIV)

Prosperity Commandment #3
Save and Invest

Worldly Habits: We get one dollar and we spend two. We get blessed with a large tax refund or settlement or other lump sum and we spend it ALL on furniture, jewelry, clothing, cars, and other frivolous items. Even worse, we get the insurance policy and six months later we're broke. Even dear old Big Mama, who remembers the days of the depression all too well, gets a day's earnings and puts it under a mattress for a rainy day – she doesn't trust the bank!

Prosperity Wisdom: God expects us to use wisdom to grow and multiply all that we are blessed to receive.

THE WORD: Understanding the Basics

Read Matthew 25: 14 – 29, The Parable of the Talents, then answer the following questions.

Matt 25: 21 and 23: What happens when you are faithful with a few things?

_____

_____

Matt 25:27: Where should the money have been placed? (NIV)

_____

_____

Matt 25:28: What happened to the money of the one who failed to increase?

_____

_____

Matt 25: 29: What happens to those who have and what happens to those who do not have (2 answers)?

_____

_____

Prov 31:16: What did the virtuous wife of Proverbs do with her earnings and why?

_____

_____

Prosperity Commandment #3
Save and Invest

THE WORD: PERFECT YOUR PROSPERITY PATH (optional)

Notes from Gen 26:12

_____

_____

Notes from Deu 1:11

_____

_____

Notes from Proverbs 13: 11 and Proverbs 21:20

_____

_____

Notes from Ecclesiastes 11:1 – 2

_____

_____

Notes from Haggai 1: 6

_____

_____

Notes from Mark 4: 8

_____

_____

Notes from Luke 19: 11 – 27

_____

_____

Prosperity Commandment #3
Save and Invest

THE WALK

1. Do you have at least $1,500 in an emergency fund?

_____

_____

2. How much do you have saved for retirement?

_____

_____

3. How many months of living expenses do you have saved outside of your retirement account?

_____

_____

4. Describe how you feel about your savings and investment strategy based on your answers to questions 1, 2, and 3 above.

_____

_____

5. Over the next seven days, open the following three accounts and begin making deposits – even if it is just $5, start somewhere:
   o Emergency Fund Account (savings account at your bank) – the goal is to get to $1500
   o Retirement Account (401k, 403b, Roth IRA, IRA, etc – if you don't have access or the minimum amount required to open either of these accounts, then open a separate account with whatever amount you can afford at your bank, contribute to it every pay period (even if it is only $5) and when you have enough, transfer this money to an official retirement account.
   o Savings/Living Expenses Account – the goal is to save 6 months of living expenses

Prosperity Commandment #3
Save and Invest

THE WISDOM:

Use this space to journal your Walk for Prosperity Commandment #3. Describe (1) what you did, (2) how it impacted others, (3) how it impacted you, and (4) what you plan to do moving forward.

(1) What you did:

_____

_____

_____

(2) How it impacted others (what happened, how did they respond):

_____

_____

_____

(3) How it impacted you (what truth, pain, joy, or freedom did you experience):

_____

_____

_____

(4) What you plan to do moving forward:

_____

_____

_____

(5) Write the scripture(s) that impacted you the most, remember it and share it with at least one other person this week.

_____

_____

_____

Living
Beyond
Check to
MONDAY

A Spiritual Path to
Wealth and Prosperity

Prosperity Commandment #4
Own Real Estate

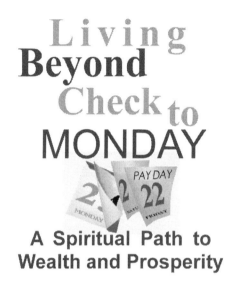

**A Spiritual Path to
Wealth and Prosperity**

*"For this is what the Lord Almighty, the God of Israel, says:
Houses, fields and vineyards will again be bought in this
land."*
(Jeremiah 32:5 NIV)

Prosperity Commandment #4
Own Real Estate

Worldly Habits: Culture has told us that when we get in a position to have, in other words "when we arrive," then we have to show the world what we have. We do that with our furniture, jewelry, name-brand clothing, electronics and cars.

Prosperity Wisdom: Land ownership is the foundation for building wealth. Land is such an important part of biblical history that wars were fought over it; lives were traded for it; and the Lord even swore an oath of land to the house of Israel. Moreover, before the Israelites were taken into Babylonian captivity, Jeremiah made strategic real estate acquisitions as a result of God's instructions.

THE WORD: Understanding the basics

Jer 32: 8 – 12: What does the Bible detail about real estate transactions?

_____

_____

Num 27: 1-7: What was the inherited item for Zelophedad's daughters?

_____

_____

Josh 23: 4 - 5: What did Joshua leave as an inheritance and what did the Lord promise to the children of Israel?

_____

_____

Ruth 4:3 – 5: What was Naomi selling, what additional item would the purchaser acquire, and why?

_____

_____

2 Sam 24: 21 - 25: What did King David buy and why did he buy it?

_____

_____

Prosperity Commandment #4
Own Real Estate

THE WORD: PERFECTING YOUR PROSPERITY PATH (optional)

Notes from Psa 37:11

_____

_____

Notes from Prov 24: 27

_____

_____

Notes from Prov 31:16

_____

_____

Prosperity Commandment #4
Own Real Estate

THE WALK – Real Estate Owners (this page is for real estate owners; those who don't own, please see the next section)

1. If you own real estate, list the addresses here:

_____

_____

2. If you own real estate, do you have an estate plan for the transfer of your wealth upon your death (remember the story of Zelophedad's daughters)?

_____

_____

3. If you own real estate, can you afford the monthly payments and if no, what are you going to do about it?

Properties I am going to keep:

_____

_____

Properties for which I am going to seek professional help in selling/disbursing:

_____

_____

4. Contact a real estate agent or broker, or a mortgage professional, to obtain a real estate acquisition analysis. You will need to acquire an ownership strategy, a market analysis, and/or a rental analysis for each property you own.

5. You have seven days to complete steps 4 and 5 above.

Prosperity Commandment #4
Own Real Estate

THE WALK – Real Estate Renters (this page is for real estate renters; those currently own, please see the previous section)

1. If you do not own real estate, how much are you currently paying for rent (or how much will you spend on rent when you graduate from school, move out of parent's home, etc.)

_____

_____

2. Multiply the amount you listed in number 1 by the number 12 and list the result below. This is how much you will spend in rent each year.

_____

_____

3. List the barriers that would prevent you from owning real estate and describe each barrier (for example, my credit is insufficient because I have $10,000 in outstanding collections or I am afraid of foreclosure):

Credit: (feel free to download the free Mortgage Approval Plan at www.lynnrichardsonloans.com)

_____

_____

Savings:

_____

_____

Income:

_____

_____

Beliefs:

_____

_____

4. You have seven days to complete steps 1 through 3 above.

Prosperity Commandment #4
Own Real Estate

THE WISDOM:

Use this space to journal your Walk for Prosperity Commandment #4. Describe (1) what you did, (2) how it impacted others, (3) how it impacted you, and (4) what you plan to do moving forward.

(1) What you did:

_____

_____

_____

(2) How it impacted others (what happened, how did they respond):

_____

_____

_____

(3) How it impacted you (what truth, pain, joy, or freedom did you experience):

_____

_____

_____

(4) What you plan to do moving forward:

_____

_____

_____

(5) Write the scripture(s) that impacted you the most, remember it and share it with at least one other person this week.

_____

_____

_____

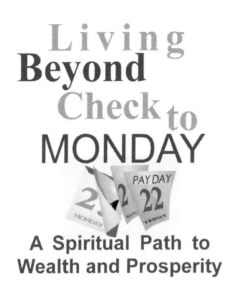

"When you ask, you do not receive, because you ask with
wrong motives, that you may spend what you get on your
pleasures."
(James 4:3 NIV)

Prosperity Commandment #5
Do Not Hoard Money and Material Possessions

Worldly Habits: We have clothing and we buy more. We have shoes and we buy more. We have electronics and we buy more. And we have the nerve to keep it all in our oversized closets and living quarters!

Prosperity Wisdom: Give away your excess so that you can make "spiritual space" for more blessings.

THE WORD: Understanding the basics
Read Luke 12:15-21 - The Parable of the Rich Fool, then answer the following questions:

Luk 12: 20 - 21: What happens to the rich man in this scripture and why?

_____

_____

Luk 12: 20: What was the reward or punishment?

_____

_____

1 Tim 6:17 – 19: What three things are the rich commanded to do and what two things are they commanded NOT to do?

_____

_____

1 John 2: 16: Where do the cravings for materials possessions come from?

_____

_____

1 Peter 1:18 – 19: What has been handed down to us? What has redeemed us?

_____

_____

Prosperity Commandment #5
Do Not Hoard Money and Material Possessions

THE WORD: PERFECTING YOUR PROSPERITY PATH (optional)

Notes from Ecclesiastes 2: 8 - 11

_____

_____

Notes from Ecclesiastes 6: 2

_____

_____

Notes from Ezekiel 28: 4 - 10

_____

_____

Notes from Matthew 6: 19 – 21

_____

_____

Notes from Luke 16: 1 - 2

_____

_____

Notes from 1 Tim 6: 9 - 10

_____

_____

Notes from James 5: 1 - 6

_____

_____

Prosperity Commandment #5
Do Not Hoard Money and Material Possessions

THE WALK

1. Complete the table below – honestly!!

Item	Quantity / Amount Owned	Is there any excess?	How Much Have I Given Away in the Past Six Months?	Who Will I Give the Excess To over the next seven days?
Shirts				
Pairs of Pants				
Pairs of Shoes				
Dresses				
Suits				
Televisions				
Cars				
Coats / Jackets				
Cash, CD's, Bank Accounts				
Computers				
List Other Items:				
List Other Items:				
List Other Items:				

2. You have seven days to complete your inventory and distribute some of the excess.

Prosperity Commandment #5
Do Not Hoard Money and Material Possessions

THE WISDOM:

Use this space to journal your Walk for Prosperity Commandment #5. Describe (1) what you did, (2) how it impacted others, (3) how it impacted you, and (4) what you plan to do moving forward.

(1) What you did:

_____

_____

_____

(2) How it impacted others (what happened, how did they respond):

_____

_____

_____

(3) How it impacted you (what truth, pain, joy, or freedom did you experience):

_____

_____

_____

(4) What you plan to do moving forward:

_____

_____

_____

(5) Write the scripture(s) that impacted you the most, remember it and share it with at least one other person this week.

_____

_____

_____

Living
Beyond
Check to
MONDAY

A Spiritual Path to
Wealth and Prosperity

Prosperity Commandment #6
Manage Creditors and Debtors Responsibly

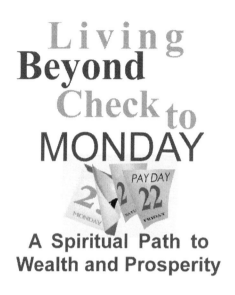

**A Spiritual Path to
Wealth and Prosperity**

*"Let no debt remain outstanding, except the continuing debt to
love one another, for he who loves his fellowman has fulfilled
the law."*
(Romans 13:8 NIV)

Prosperity Commandment #6
Manage Creditors and Debtors Responsibly

Worldly Habits: We spend out of temptation and desire and we take loans for the simplest of things. Every time we use a charge card for a new pair of shoes, we are taking out a loan! At the same time, we owe others and do not pay them, but we have the nerve to treat those who owe us money with an unforgiving heart.

Prosperity Wisdom: Understand that credit is a gift, not a right. Apply the golden rule: treat your creditors as you would have your debtors treat you.

THE WORD: Understanding the Basics

Read Matthew 18: 23 – 35 then answer the questions below:

Matthew 18: 26 - 27: What should you do when you owe someone?

_____

_____

Matthew 18: 28 – 34: What happened to the creditor who treated his debtor unfairly?

_____

_____

Ezekiel 18: 7 – 9: What credit/debt attributes are illustrated here? What happens to this man?

_____

_____

Ezekiel 18: 12 – 13: What credit/debt attributes are illustrated here? What happens to this man?

_____

_____

Proverbs 22:1: What should be more desirable than wealth?

_____

_____

Deu 24: 10 – 13: How should we treat our debtors?

_____

_____

Prosperity Commandment #6
Manage Creditors and Debtors Responsibly

THE WORD: Understanding the Basics (continued)

Rom 13: 6 - 7: What should we give to everyone (verse 7)?

_____

_____

Rom 13: 8: What is the only debt that should remain outstanding?

_____

_____

2 Corinthians 5: 10: What does this scripture imply as it relates to credit and debt?

_____

_____

Prosperity Commandment #6
Manage Creditors and Debtors Responsibly

THE WORD: PERFECTING YOUR PROSPERITY PATH (optional):

Notes from Deu 15: 1 – 6

_____

_____

Notes from Psalm 15:4

_____

_____

Notes from Psalm 37: 21

_____

_____

Notes from Prov 22: 7

_____

_____

Notes from Proverbs 22: 26

_____

_____

Notes from Ecclesiastes 5: 4 - 5

_____

_____

Notes from Ecclesiastes 7:1

_____

_____

Prosperity Commandment #6
Manage Creditors and Debtors Responsibly

THE WORD: PERFECTING YOUR PROSPERITY PATH (optional):

Notes from Matthew 7:12

_____

_____

Notes from Matthew 22: 15 – 22

_____

_____

Notes from Luke 7: 41 – 43

_____

_____

Notes from Luke 16: 1 – 2 and 10 – 13

_____

_____

Notes from James 4: 2 – 3

_____

_____

Prosperity Commandment #6
Manage Creditors and Debtors Responsibly

THE WALK – OBSERVE YOUR SPENDING

1. Track your spending for fourteen days. Take this book with you everywhere you go. List each and every expense in the column below the corresponding date. List each and every atm withdrawal. Check your account at the beginning of each day to see what has been deducted the previous day so you will not overlook any expenses. *Ex: light bill $175.09; Coffee: $5.98; daughter's field trip $10*

Day 1:	Day 2:	Day 3:	Day 4:	Day 5:	Day 6:	Day 7:
Ex: Coffee $1.79						

Prosperity Commandment #6
Manage Creditors and Debtors Responsibly

THE WALK – OBSERVE YOUR SPENDING

1. Continue to track your spending . . . Take this book with you everywhere you go. List each and every expense in the column below the corresponding date. List each and every atm withdrawal. Check your account at the beginning of each day to see what has been deducted the previous day so you will not overlook any expenses.

Day 8:	Day 9:	Day 10:	Day 11:	Day 12:	Day 13:	Day 14:

Prosperity Commandment #6
Manage Creditors and Debtors Responsibly

THE WALK – OBSERVE YOUR SPENDING

2. After you track your spending for fourteen days . . . you will surely be aware of some areas where you can decrease or eliminate your spending. Review the list and record the items below that you will either eliminate or minimize:

Item	Current Expense over 14 days	Is this a need or a want?	New Expense
Lunch	$178.98	Need / but I can minimize	$0 – bringing my lunch

Prosperity Commandment #6
Manage Creditors and Debtors Responsibly

THE WALK – MANAGING YOUR INCOME AND EXPENSES: This may include making some tough financial decisions like increasing your income, destroying your credit cards, taking your lunch to work, consolidating you debt, suspending extracurricular activities, or even filing for bankruptcy.

Use the space below . . . and take your time. Remember, you cannot fix what you will not face. Getting a handle on what you have going out is a critical step to establishing peace within and control over your financial situation.

3. List all of your monthly Income and Expenses in the chart below.

	Income Source	Monthly Amount
1		
2		
3		
4		
5	TOTAL MONTHLY INCOME	
	Creditor	**Monthly Amount**
Ex	*Mortgage – every month*	*1200*
Ex	*Life Insurance – $300 every quarter*	*200*
Ex	*Auto Insurance $600 every 6 months*	*100*
Ex	*Membership Dues $600 once a year*	*50*
6	Tithes	
7	Saving / Investing	
8	Rent / 1st Mortgage Payments	
9	Renters /HomeOwners Insurance (do not list if included in #1 above)	
10	Real Estate Taxes (do not list here if included in #1 above)	
11	Car Notes	
12	Car Insurance	
13	Life Insurance	
14	Child Support / Alimony	
15	Home Telephone Bill	
16	Cable Bill	
17	Gas Bill	
18	Electric Bill	
19	Internet Service	
20	Cell Phone Bills	
21	Water bill	
22	Landscaping	
23	Waste Management (do not include if included in #19)	
24	Total Student Loans	
25	Total Credit Cards:	
26	Other:	
27	Other:	
28	Other:	
29	**TOTAL MONTHLY EXPENSES**	
30	**Subtract line 29 from line 5**	
	If you have a negative number, you MUST minimize some expenses	

Don't forget to list those other hidden "bills", for example: kids activities; club memberships; dvd club; memberships; health club memberships

Prosperity Commandment #6
Manage Creditors and Debtors Responsibly

THE WALK – MANAGING YOUR CREDITORS

4. Visit www.annualcreditreport.com and order all three of your credit reports. You may also visit www.truecredit.com to receive all three reports at one time as well as your credit scores. List the date you complete this task below. Print it out and place a copy in this book.

---

5. In the top half of the table below, list all of your current creditors with the lowest balance first and continue until you get to the highest balance. In the lower half, list your past due collections / charge-offs / judgments and begin the process of paying them off and/or disputing them with the appropriate credit bureau:

Current Creditor	Balance Due	Current Monthly Payment	New Monthly Payment
Collections / Judgments	Amount Reported by Equifax	Amount Reported by Experian	Amount Reported by Transunion

If you have ANY EXTRA MONEY, first pay off your collections (start with the smallest one first). After that, add any extra money to the first debt on your list and write your new monthly payment. Pay that debt off. After that debt is paid off, then take all of the money from that debt and apply it to the next debt on your list and write in your new monthly payment. You will have to revisit this section until all of your bills are paid (see www.lynnrichardson.com for the automated debt reduction plan).

Prosperity Commandment #6
Manage Creditors and Debtors Responsibly

THE WALK – MANAGING YOUR DEBTORS

6. List everyone who owes you money and how much they owe you.

Debtor Name	Balance Due	Monthly Payment Requested	Is this a Gift?

6a. Write the following letter to each and every one of your debtors and mail it to them:

Dear Debtor:

On _____ I loaned you _____ dollars and you promised to repay it by _____. I understand that circumstances may have prevented you from paying; however, we have communicated to discuss how this debt will be satisfied. Trust me when I tell you that I understand how embarrassing it is to borrow and not be able to repay. I kindly ask that you call me or email me or write me back and propose a repayment plan. In the meantime, know that God loves you and I am praying for peace in your finances.

6b. If you receive a repayment plan, list the amount in the table above.

6c. If there is no response or if you are led to do so, write the debt off as a "Gift" by making the proper notation in last column in the table.

7. You have seven days to complete steps 1 through 6c above.

Prosperity Commandment #6
Manage Creditors and Debtors Responsibly

THE WISDOM:

Use this space to journal your Walk for Prosperity Commandment #6. Describe (1) what you did, (2) how it impacted others, (3) how it impacted you, and (4) what you plan to do moving forward.

(1) What you did:

_____

_____

_____

(2) How it impacted others (what happened, how did they respond):

_____

_____

_____

(3) How it impacted you (what truth, pain, joy, or freedom did you experience):

_____

_____

_____

(4) What you plan to do moving forward:

_____

_____

_____

(5) Write the scripture(s) that impacted you the most, remember it and share it with at least one other person this week.

_____

_____

_____

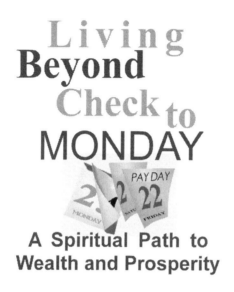

A Spiritual Path to
Wealth and Prosperity

"A good man leaves an inheritance for his children's children."
(Proverbs 13:22 NIV)

Prosperity Commandment #7
Leave an Inheritance

Worldly Habits: We accumulate assets with no regard for future generations. I have often heard the phrase "since nobody helped me, then why should we help anyone else?" For those of us who have no heirs, children or loved ones that we would want to take care of after our death, we do not believe that inheritance planning is relevant and/or important.

Prosperity Wisdom: We should use our wisdom and resources to benefit God's Kingdom for the fulfillment of His Will now and in the future.

THE WORD: Understanding the Basics

Genesis: 25: 5: Who is the beneficiary of Abraham's possessions?

_____

_____

Exodus 6: 1 – 8: What did God promise to Abraham, Isaac, and Jacob?

_____

_____

Numbers 27: 5 – 11: What does scripture tell us about the protocol for inheritances?

_____

_____

John 3: 16: What have we inherited as a result of the sacrifice of Jesus?

_____

_____

What can we do to pass this inheritance on as noted in Numbers 27: 5 – 11?

_____

_____

Prosperity Commandment #7
Leave an Inheritance

PERFECTING YOUR PROSPERITY PATH: (optional)

Notes from Numbers 36: 7 – 8

_____

_____

Notes from Josh 1: 6 and Josh 23: 4 – 5

_____

_____

Notes from 1 Kings 21: 2 – 4

_____

_____

Notes from Job 42:15

_____

_____

Notes from Psalm 115:14

_____

_____

Notes from Proverbs 13:22

_____

_____

Prosperity Commandment #7
Leave an Inheritance

THE WALK

1. List the value of your assets below:

Asset / Item	Value	Who will inherit this item?
Furniture		
Jewelry		
Clothing		
Automobile		
Real Estate		
Pension		
Insurance Policies		
Other Assets		
Cash / Checking / Savings		

2. Schedule an appointment with an estate planning attorney or financial planner to properly document your wishes as noted above.

Appointment Date:

Name of Estate Planning Professional:

3. You have seven days to complete steps 1 and 2 above.

Prosperity Commandment #7
Leave an Inheritance

THE WISDOM:

Use this space to journal your Walk for Prosperity Commandment #7. Describe (1) what you did, (2) how it impacted others, (3) how it impacted you, and (4) what you plan to do moving forward.

(1) What you did:

_____

_____

_____

(2) How it impacted others (what happened, how did they respond):

_____

_____

_____

(3) How it impacted you (what truth, pain, joy, or freedom did you experience):

_____

_____

_____

(4) What you plan to do moving forward:

_____

_____

_____

(5) Write the scripture(s) that impacted you the most, remember it and share it with at least one other person this week.

_____

_____

_____

Living Beyond Check to MONDAY

A Spiritual Path to Wealth and Prosperity

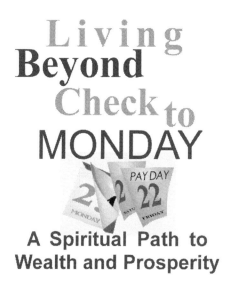

Living
Beyond
Check to
MONDAY

**A Spiritual Path to
Wealth and Prosperity**

" . . . If a man will not work he shall not eat."
(2 Thessalonians 3:10 NIV)

Prosperity Commandment #8
Develop Multiple Streams of Income

Worldly Habits: We have been taught to go to school, get a good job and retire into the sunset. Or even worse, many of us rely on faith alone to achieve our goals and dreams. All too often we put all of our eggs in one basket and when the basket is empty – we don't eat!

Prosperity Wisdom: Utilize the talents and gifts you have been given to gather provision while being an asset to the world around you.

THE WORD: Understanding the Basics

Prov 31: 10 - 31: List the jobs (paid and unpaid) of the virtuous wife. How many of those jobs generated revenue?

_____

_____

Luke 16: 1 – 8: What did the manager do when he found out he was losing his job?

_____

_____

James 2: 14 – 26: What is required in addition to faith to achieve what God has for you?

_____

_____

Prosperity Commandment #8
Develop Multiple Streams of Income

THE WORD: PERFECTING YOUR PROSPERITY PATH (optional)

Notes from Jeremiah 29:11

_____

_____

Notes from 1 Chronicles 4: 9 – 10

_____

_____

Notes from Matthew 7: 7 – 8

_____

_____

Notes from 1 Corinthians 12: 4 – 12

_____

_____

Notes from Ephesians 3:20

_____

_____

Notes from 2 Thessalonians 3: 7 - 12:

_____

_____

Prosperity Commandment #8
Develop Multiple Streams of Income

SCRIPTURE REVIEW OF WORK ETHIC

Notes from Deuteronomy 24: 14 - 15

_____

_____

Notes from Proverbs 16:26

_____

_____

Notes from Proverbs 17:20; Proverbs 18:9

_____

_____

Notes from Proverbs 20:4

_____

_____

Notes from Proverbs 20:13 and v 17

_____

_____

Notes from Proverbs 21: 5 – 6 and v 25

_____

_____

Notes from Luke 12: 42 - 48

_____

_____

Notes from Colossians 3:23

_____

_____

Prosperity Commandment #8
Develop Multiple Streams of Income

THE WALK

1. Complete the Multiple Streams of Income Table Below

Current Source of Income	How Often Do I receive this Income and how much do I receive?	What unexpected or unfortunate event could end this stream of income?

2. Assess your back-up plan in the event there is an interruption of income from one or more of the sources above:

Current Source of Income	What Do you have in Place that would Guarantee immediate replacement of this income?	If you were to lose this income, approximately how long would it take for you to restore this stream of income?

Prosperity Commandment #8
Develop Multiple Streams of Income

3. Complete your Multiple Stream of Income Strategy:

Current Talent, Gift, or Resource that is not generating income	How Can You use this Talent or Gift to Create and Income Stream?	List three things you can do within the next thirty days in order to implement this stream of income

4. You have seven days to complete steps 1 through 3 above.

Prosperity Commandment #8
Develop Multiple Streams of Income

THE WISDOM:

Use this space to journal your Walk for Prosperity Commandment #8. Describe (1) what you did, (2) how it impacted others, (3) how it impacted you, and (4) what you plan to do moving forward.

(1) What you did:

_____

_____

_____

(2) How it impacted others (what happened, how did they respond):

_____

_____

_____

(3) How it impacted you (what truth, pain, joy, or freedom did you experience):

_____

_____

_____

(4) What you plan to do moving forward:

_____

_____

_____

(5) Write the scripture(s) that impacted you the most, remember it and share it with at least one other person this week.

_____

_____

_____

Living
Beyond
Check to
MONDAY

A Spiritual Path to
Wealth and Prosperity

Prosperity Commandment # 9
Seek Wise Counsel on Financial Matters

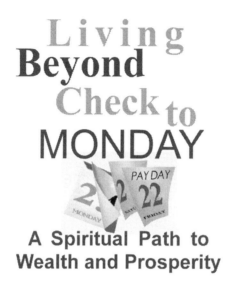

A Spiritual Path to Wealth and Prosperity

"Plans fail for lack of counsel, but with many advisers they succeed."
(Proverbs 15:22 NIV)

Prosperity Commandment # 9
Seek Wise Counsel on Financial Matters

Worldly Habits: We are either too proud or too ignorant, or both, to ask for help in areas where we are deficient. We would rather "prove" to everyone that we can succeed than seek advise from those who have already been where we are trying to go.

Prosperity Wisdom: Wisdom is supreme; therefore get wisdom. Though it cost all you have, get understanding. (Prov: 4:7 NIV)

THE WORD: Understanding the Basics

Prov 17:16: What does this scripture imply about someone who has money but has no wisdom?

_____

_____

Prov 8: 10 – 11: What should you seek that has more value than money and riches?

_____

_____

1 Cor 9:25: What is required of everyone who competes and expects to win?

_____

_____

Proverbs 11:14: What ensures victory?

_____

_____

Proverbs 13: 18: What two things befall those who ignore discipline?

_____

_____

Joshua 1: 8: What should you do if you want to achieve success and prosperity?

_____

_____

Prosperity Commandment # 9
Seek Wise Counsel on Financial Matters

THE WORD: PERFECTING YOUR PROSPERITY (optional)

Notes from 1Kings 12: 6 – 20

_____

_____

Notes from Prov 8: 12 – 25

_____

_____

Notes from Prov 16: 16 - 18

_____

_____

Notes from Ecc 9:16

_____

_____

Notes from John 16:13 - 15

_____

_____

Prosperity Commandment # 9
Seek Wise Counsel on Financial Matters

THE WALK

1. With whom do you consult for at least one hour per month on financial matters?

_____

_____

2. Do you have a written and identifiable plan in place to help you achieve **all** of the following:

    1) Sufficient income for giving, saving and spending;

        Yes   or   No

    2) A life of debt free living;

        Yes   or   No

    3) Sufficient income, land and resources during retirement

        Yes   or   No

    4) A plan to disperse your wealth after your death

        Yes   or   No

Prosperity Commandment # 9
Seek Wise Counsel on Financial Matters

3. List at least 2 potential advisors/professionals in each category to help you achieve your goals (you will contact each advisor and schedule a face to face appointment):

Goal	Advisor 1 (name and phone) And Appointment	Advisor 2 (name and phone) And Appointment Date
Financial Planning, budgeting, saving, retirement		
A real estate maintenance or acquisition strategy		
Credit Building		
A plan to disperse my possession after my death and leave an inheritance		
Spiritual Covering	List Your Spiritual Advisor Here	List a 2nd Spiritual Advisor Here

4. You have seven days to complete steps 1 through 3 above (appointments must be scheduled; not necessarily completed).

Prosperity Commandment # 9
Seek Wise Counsel on Financial Matters

THE WISDOM:

Use this space to journal your Walk for Prosperity Commandment #9. Describe (1) what you did, (2) how it impacted others, (3) how it impacted you, and (4) what you plan to do moving forward.

(1) What you did:

_____

_____

_____

(2) How it impacted others (what happened, how did they respond):

_____

_____

_____

(3) How it impacted you (what truth, pain, joy, or freedom did you experience):

_____

_____

_____

(4) What you plan to do moving forward:

_____

_____

_____

(5) Write the scripture(s) that impacted you the most, remember it and share it with at least one other person this week.

_____

_____

_____

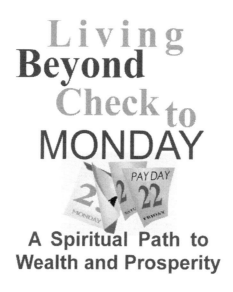

Living
Beyond
Check to
MONDAY

**A Spiritual Path to
Wealth and Prosperity**

*"Honor the Lord with your wealth, with the first fruits of all
your crops; then your barns will be filled to overflowing, and
your vats will brim over with new wine."*
(Proverbs 3:10 NIV)

Prosperity Commandment # 10
Tithe Faithfully

Worldly Habits: We operate with a "when I" attitude. When I make more money I will tithe. When I find the right church I will tithe. When I understand why I should tithe I will tithe.

Prosperity Wisdom: You must have faith and believe that God, who owns everything, will provide for your needs. Faith in the form of tithing is a perquisite for manifesting all that faith releases in our lives.

THE WORD: Understanding the Basics

Psalm 24: 1-2 and Deu 10:14 What belongs to God?

_____

_____

Malachi 3: 8: How do we rob God?

_____

_____

Proverbs 3:9: What two ways do we honor God?

_____

_____

Malachi 3: 10 - 12: What three things will happen if you are obedient with your tithing?

_____

_____

_____

Judges 6:16 - 18: What did Gideon indicate he would bring when he wanted to know if it was really God speaking to him? And what did God say he would do?

_____

_____

Prosperity Commandment # 10
Tithe Faithfully

THE WORD: PERFECTING YOUR PROSPERITY PATH (optional)

Notes on Gen 14:18 – 20 and Hebrews 6:20, Hebrews 7:1 – 10
(What references can you draw? Answer this question: Is tithing just an Old Testament Law of the Books of Moses, or did it precede Moses?)

_____

_____

_____

Notes on Deuteronomy 14: 22 - 29

_____

_____

Notes on Deuteronomy 16:16

_____

_____

Notes on 2 Chronicles 31: v5 and v12

_____

_____

Notes on Ecclesiastes 11: 1 - 2

_____

_____

Notes on Ezekiel 20:40

_____

_____

Notes on Matt 23:23 and 1 Cor 16:2

_____

Prosperity Commandment # 10
Tithe Faithfully

THE WALK

1. List your total monthly take home pay (if you are self-employed, list your average monthly pay):

_____

_____

2. List ten percent of your total monthly take home pay (this is your tithing commitment):

_____

_____

3. List the additional amount you will contribute to offerings on a monthly basis.

_____

_____

4. Do you believe you can "afford" to commit to items 2 and 3 above? _____

If the answer is yes, then proceed to Commandment #10.   If the answer is no, take a look at your spending diary from Prosperity Commandment # 6 and list what items you will eliminate in order to commit to 2 and 3 above.

_____

_____

5. You have seven days to complete steps 1 through 4 above.

Prosperity Commandment # 10
Tithe Faithfully

THE WISDOM:

Use this space to journal your Walk for Prosperity Commandment #10. Describe (1) what you did, (2) how it impacted others, (3) how it impacted you, and (4) what you plan to do moving forward.

(1) What you did:

_____

_____

_____

(2) How it impacted others (what happened, how did they respond):

_____

_____

_____

(3) How it impacted you (what truth, pain, joy, or freedom did you experience):

_____

_____

_____

(4) What you plan to do moving forward:

_____

_____

_____

(5) Write the scripture(s) that impacted you the most, remember it and share it with at least one other person this week.

_____

_____

_____

Living Beyond Check to MONDAY

A Spiritual Path to Wealth and Prosperity

Part 4

Your Daily Walk

This is a lot to take in. Some of us are impatient: now that we have seen the face of God and have turned from our ways, we want God to deliver us RIGHT NOW from our financial mess. But it took time to get into the financial mess we are in and it will take prayer, obedience, discipline, and time to get us out. As I say to my friends . . . "it's going to take a lot of undoing to undo all of the doing we have done!"

Along this path, you are bound to face contradictions to what God has promised. These contradictions are manifested through fear, worry, temptation and pride.

This section outlines your daily walk. If you remember these principles daily, you will achieve the prosperity that is in store for you.

Your Daily Walk

Read this section each day for one year on your path to wealth and prosperity.

1.   FATHER: GOD HAS WEALTH IN MIND FOR YOU

Wealthy people are not disqualified from achieving everlasting life in Christ. However as Joyce Meyers said in one of her sermons "each and every one of us must past two tests in order to achieve true wealth and prosperity: 1. What we do when we don't have enough money; 2. What we do when we have more than enough money." God has prosperity in mind for you, but until you pass the test you cannot go to the next wealth grade. Be reminded of the following fathers in faith who received their wealth and prosperity from the Heavenly Father.

Notes on Abraham in Gen 13:2

_____

_____

_____

Notes on Job in Job 42:12

_____

_____

_____

Notes on Isaac in Gen 26: 12 – 14

_____

_____

_____

Notes on Solomon in 1 Kings 3: 13 – 14

_____

_____

_____

Read this section each day for one year on your path to wealth and prosperity.

2.   THE SON: JESUS COMMANDS US NOT TO WORRY

*R*emember **this section of scripture every time you are tempted to worry or experience anxiety about money.**

Matthew 6: 25 – 33 (NIV)

25"Therefore I tell you, do not worry about your life, what you will eat or drink; or about your body, what you will wear. Is not life more important than food, and the body more important than clothes? 26 Look at the birds of the air; they do not sow or reap or store away in barns, and yet your heavenly Father feeds them. Are you not much more valuable than they? 27 Who of you by worrying can add a single hour to his life[a]? 28 And why do you worry about clothes? See how the lilies of the field grow. They do not labor or spin. 29Yet I tell you that not even Solomon in all his splendor was dressed like one of these. 30If that is how God clothes the grass of the field, which is here today and tomorrow is thrown into the fire, will he not much more clothe you, O you of little faith? 31So do not worry, saying, 'What shall we eat?' or 'What shall we drink?' or 'What shall we wear?' 32For the pagans run after all these things, and your heavenly Father knows that you need them. 33But seek first his kingdom and his righteousness, and all these things will be given to you as well. 34Therefore do not worry about tomorrow, for tomorrow will worry about itself. Each day has enough trouble of its own.

List your worries on another sheet of paper, every day after you read this section, then safely burn / or discard the paper. Do this each day, listing the items daily, until the items are no longer a worry for you.

Read this section each day for one year on your path to wealth and prosperity.

3.   THE HOLY SPIRIT: ALLOW IT TO DWELL IN YOU

1 Corinthians 2: 14 - 16

The man without the Spirit does not accept the things that come from the Spirit of God, for they are foolishness to him, and he cannot understand them, because they are spiritually discerned. The spiritual man makes judgments about all things, but he himself is not subject to any man's judgment.

List any areas for which you are seeking an increase in spiritual discernment:

_____

_____

_____

_____

_____

Jeremiah 29: 11 - 13

"For I know the plans I have for you," declares the LORD, "plans to prosper you and not to harm you, plans to give you hope and a future. Then you will call upon me and come and pray to me, and I will listen to you. You will seek me and find me when you seek me with all your heart."

List your perception of the Lord's plan for you and/or list the areas for which you are seeking clarity:

_____

_____

_____

_____

_____

My Testimony

I remember that period in my life. I had been living from check to Monday. Not check to check – check to Monday. You see, living from check to check means you have enough money to last until payday and <u>then</u> you're broke. Living check to Monday is a whole different game. You get paid on Friday, kick it on the weekend, pay on your past due bills, and on Monday, you're broke.

And I was making over $20,000 a month. The problem was, however, my business and personal bills were $30,000, or maybe more – I didn't really know because I had been making hundreds of thousands of dollars annually for years and my solution for not having ENOUGH money was to work harder and longer to make MORE money. I thought budgets were for poor people! Sad . . . but true.

When my "saved" friends would tell me to pray for a solution to my money dilemma, I would say, "if Jesus didn't put any money in the mailbox TODAY, I don't know what PRAYING will do for me!"

I was destitute, down and out, and broken. Every person I had helped, every person I had given money to, every person I had "saved" financially when I was doing well had turned their backs on me, including some of my relatives. The worst part was I felt like a big hypocrite, and I was -- teaching everybody else about wealth, even wrote a book about it, and there I was, totally jacked up.

I had no more money and therefore, nothing to hide behind. I used to think I "gave" money to Pookie, Ray-Ray, friends and family members because I was saving them. I convinced myself that I had a good heart and that my "giving" to others was evidence of my Christianity. But I know now that I was really feeding my own pride. I was reinforcing my ability to control others; moreover, I was enabling others to be co-dependent on me and then I had the nerve to get an attitude about the co-dependency I had helped create.

But when I had no more money and could no longer fake it -- I finally realized I had no one left but God. I had personally decided I was mentally ill. Then I decided I was just too embarrassed and down and out to face life, people, situations, and my poor financial condition. I couldn't end it all because I was too much of a coward to actually do anything to myself. So I told God that if he saved me from myself, if he helped me get out of my situation, if he gave me yet another chance, then anybody and everybody who knew me, would have an opportunity to know God. I promised that those who saw me, would see that God is real because His spirit would be in me.

And I was transformed. The scripture that reminds me of how loving and merciful God is, is ***Psalms 118:5 (NIV): "In my anguish, I cried to the Lord and He answered by setting me free."*** I feel as if God personally reached down and pulled me out of that state of mind, that life, and gave me another.

Although I cry when think back on that time, I am crying for a different reason now.

My Testimony

Now I cry with a heart of gratitude and a peace that surpasses all understanding. I often look at people who are lost and I just want to cut a piece of my heart and give it to them so they will know what a heart that loves and fears God feels like. I want them to have what I have, but I also remember I was once where they are so instead of getting mad, and acting "holy and righteous," I pray. I pray that they will no longer be blind to the light of Jesus. I pray that they will just trust God enough to give their lives, completely, to Him. I pray that the love, lust or lack of money will cease to be the puppet strings in the lives of others.

And this is where my part of the deal kicks in.

I promised God that when people saw me, they would see Him. I try to live up to that promise in my daily walk. I try to live up to that promise in my business dealings, my family dealings, when I discipline my children, when I disagree with my husband, and yes, when I make decisions about money.

Now, don't get me wrong. I have been tested. I was all set to go to the biggest event of the century -- the biggest event of my lifetime. I had my airline ticket and invitations to some of the most notable balls and events: it was the inauguration of President Barack Obama. I know people who would have sold all of their possessions and their kids too, just to be in the presence of history being made. I made the decision not to go. Why? Because it was not in my budget. The Holy Spirit told me that there were higher priorities, and I had a choice to make. First I talked to my husband. Then I read the Bible. Then I made the decision to stay home. Then . . . I cried and I wept, and I wept and I cried. My ego and my pride kept telling me that I was SUPPOSED to be there! But I stuck to my decision. And after a day or so, I was okay. I can even laugh about it now (but not too much!!!!).

And this is where your part of the deal kicks in.

You, too, will have decisions to make. You, too, will have to give up some things. You, like me, and like everyone else on this path, will have to make some unpopular decisions and "Others" are going to try to convince you to do what the Holy Spirit has instructed you NOT to do, and vice versa.

So, beware! "Others" come in familiar clothing and with smiling faces: children (especially the baby!), loved ones, family, friends, addictions, and all kinds of situations. But you must stand in your truth and understand that when the Holy Spirit is with you, it is impossible to fail.

I have passed the torch to you. It is now your responsibility to take this daily walk . . . this Spiritual Path to Wealth and Prosperity . . . and pass the torch to others in your family, community, and world.

Your Testimony

Your Testimony

_____

_____

_____

_____

_____

_____

_____

_____

_____

_____

_____

_____

_____

_____

_____

_____

_____

_____

About the Author

_K_nown to thousands as "The Mortgage Guru," and named by Urban Influence Magazine as one of the 20 hottest influencers in America, Lynn Richardson is more than just another real estate professional helping families achieve the American dream. The author, broadcaster and motivational speaker uses her quick wit and humorous presentation style to help others face their money issues and achieve personal, professional, and spiritual harmony. The recipient of countless awards and featured in numerous media outlets (Essence, Jet, Upscale, Tom Joyner Morning Show, etc.), Lynn is the Chief Operating Executive of the Hip-Hop Summit Action Network (www.hsan.org), where she works closely with co-founders Russell Simmons and Dr. Benjamin Chavis, as well as a host of A-list celebrities, to execute the organization's empowerment programs that impact the global hip-hop community.

With more than a decade of leading roles in the banking and real estate sales industries, Lynn became a national figure after closing more than 100 million in mortgages for urban families, most notably a lady with 4 bankruptcies and 2 foreclosures who became a homeowner after following Lynn's signature Mortgage Approval Plan (MAP), which is now used by industry professionals nationwide. A former Vice President for JP Morgan Chase, Lynn increased the outcome of the Delta Sigma Theta Homeownership initiative by over 389% and later implemented the Alpha Kappa Alpha Keys to Homeownership initiative. Lynn further expanded her influence by creating and partnering with State Farm / Ian Smith's 50 Million Pound Challenge on the HBCU Health, Wealth 'n Real Estate Tour.

Lynn's vision is best portrayed in her books, most notably Living Check to Monday: The Real Deal About Money, Credit and Financial Security, which achieved Best Seller status at the 2008 Congressional Black Caucus Conference Book Pavilion. Yes! You're Approved: The Real Deal About Getting a Mortgage and Buying a Home, and Put On Your Financial Armor: End Your Battle with Money for Good were released in 2009 and 2010, respectively.

A member of Delta Sigma Theta Sorority, the National Association of Real Estate Brokers, and Jack and Jill of America, Lynn received her undergraduate education at Northwestern University and Loyola University. She is currently pursuing a Master of Arts in Urban Ministry at Trinity International University, is a faithful member at New Faith Baptist Church International, has been married for fifteen years to her best friend, Demietrius, and is the mother of three beautiful daughters.